Rainf

MW01028448

Written by Sarah O'Neil
Photography by Michael Curtain

This is a rainforest.
Many plants grow in a rainforest.

Some rainforest plants get a
lot of sunlight.
Some rainforest plants do not get
a lot of sunlight.

4

This is the floor of the rainforest.
It's at the bottom of the forest.
Very little sunlight gets
to the rainforest floor.

5

Small plants and moss grow
on the rainforest floor.
They do not get a lot of sunlight.

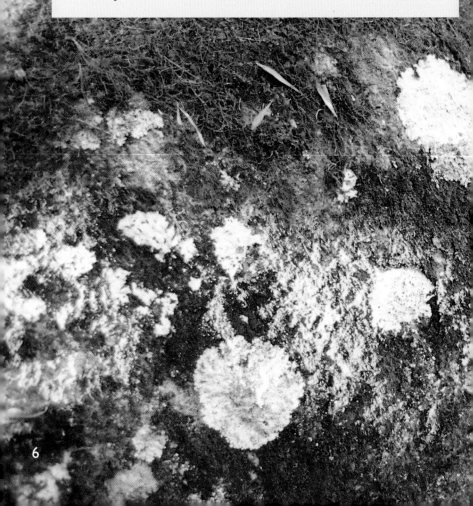

Ferns grow on the rainforest floor.
They do not get a lot of sunlight.

9

These small trees, plants, and vines grow higher up in the rainforest.
They get more sunlight.

11

These big trees grow
to the top of the rainforest.
They get a lot of sunlight.

This tree has grown taller than all the other plants in the rainforest. It gets the most sunlight.

Plants at the top of the rainforest get lots of sunlight.

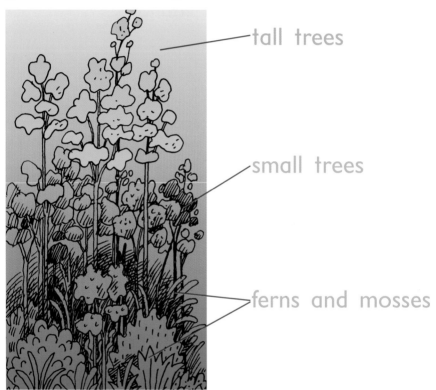

tall trees

small trees

ferns and mosses

Plants near the rainforest floor get very little sunlight.